To Bobby
You will grow
to New heights!
Cynthia

FINANCIAL BAILOUT

A GUIDE TO CREATING YOUR OWN FINANCIAL RESCUE PLAN AND NAVIGATING YOUR WAY TO FINANCIAL SECURITY DURING A RECESSION.

Cynthia E. Nevels

AuthorHouse™
1663 Liberty Drive
Bloomington, IN 47403
www.authorhouse.com
Phone: 1-800-839-8640

First published by AuthorHouse 7/28/2009

ISBN: 978-1-4389-9231-0 (e)
ISBN: 978-1-4389-9230-3 (sc)

Printed in the United States of America
Bloomington, Indiana

This book is printed on acid-free paper.

Dedication

This book is dedicated to my money smart and loving children who inspire me each day. Thank you Jeremy, Tyler, and Miachel.

TABLE OF CONTENTS

Foreword

This book addresses an urgent need for women during a difficult time in the history of our country. While most families have been affected by the deep recession and banking crisis of the past year and a half, I share Cynthia's concern about women and their financial recovery. In my nearly three decades as a financial advisor at Merrill Lynch, I have focused on empowering women of all ages and backgrounds around money. In my experiences, I have seen firsthand the obstacles women face in their quest for financial security. All women need a financial recovery plan at a time like this. My more affluent clients are looking for ways to maintain their standard of living and preserve what they have. They feel as much fear as those who have much less. We're all in this same emotional place.

Whether it is the 75-year-old woman who is newly widowed and has never written a check in her life; the recently divorced 56-year-old woman who raised the children, ran the home and has neither a marketable skill nor adequate assets and must now make her own way; or the single mother with young children and no other means of support, I've worked with many women from several walks of life and all in difficult financial situations. These women — and likely several of you reading — have had to overcome huge deficits in order to gain and maintain financial security.

As I like to say in my "Women are Money" classes, "I've got good news and bad news. The bad news is that we are all personally responsible for creating our own financial freedom. The good news is that we are all personally responsible for creating own financial freedom." Of course, that's tongue in cheek. Still, when we take that statement to heart, it's empowering. Think about it, there's no one else who can do a job as well as you, right? There you go, knock yourself out!

One of the attributes I love most about women is our sheer tenacity honed from centuries of successful focus and multitasking. Taking care of house and home, children, parents and even pets is second nature to us. We come up short, however, when it comes to taking care of ourselves and planning our financial futures. As women, it is our intrinsic need to put others first and our strong desire to keep the peace. I have spent countless hours trying to convince women that being passive about the money issues in their homes is actually an active choice that leaves their financial destiny squarely in the hands of someone else. Ninety-six percent of those women about whom I speak will end up in charge of their own finances in their lifetimes, however, for many it will come at a point when life mandates: the loss of loved ones, sudden loss of income, and career or divorce.

As a gender, we were poorly prepared for the responsibility of personal money management even before the recent drastic downturn in the economy. Now, we must take hold for ourselves. In reading this book, you have taken one step closer to realizing your financial dream. Why? Because you have challenged yourself to become educated on financial topics as they pertain to you. Below, I have outlined nuggets that I share with my clients as "Dos" and "Don'ts" to securing their financial futures.

The "Do's":

- Take personal responsibility for achieving financial goals
- Get professional help
- Start from this point
- Spend less than you make
- Use debt wisely
- Teach your kids fiscal responsibility
- Cover your big risks first
- Take baby steps
- Expect the best and plan for the worst

The "Don'ts":

- Spend time on "ifs and buts"
- Pay others before paying yourself (spending vs. saving)
- Procrastinate
- Blame others for your situation
- Give up – there are *always* choices

Cynthia's book provides concise timely information and a roadmap for devising your own financial recovery plan. The concepts presented here are pertinent to all of us, regardless of our social class, age, ethnicity, or marital status. Know that what you read here, you *can do.* Then challenge yourself to make these pages your reality.

Helen Wathen CFP® CIMA®

Vice President

Wealth Management Advisor

Merrill Lynch

Overview

The dramatic changes taking place in the financial services industry and the economy are historic in scope and proportion. Job loss is prevalent, the credit crisis is crippling, and the home foreclosure crisis is disturbing. Historically, women have been slow to protect their assets in both good and bad economic climates, which may leave them vulnerable when it comes to wealth management. The Financial Bailout will explain current economic challenges, will become show how the government bailout plan will affect women, and will serve as a practical instruction guide on what to do to protect your assets. The Financial Bailout will review areas of vulnerability weak due to the current financial uncertainty, explore personal financial negligence, and witness the effects a recession will have on a woman's future retirement. In addition, the guide will reveal steps to assess the damage, hire the right professional, rebuild what was lost, and acquire more resources to mitigate future exposure and financial vulnerability. In the March

2009 Fawcett Report, Dr. Katherine Rake, OBE reports that women are more directly exposed to the impact of this recession as employees than they were in the recessions of the 1990s or 1980s. She argues that the fact that women have entered this recession on an unequal economic footing makes them particularly vulnerable to the impact of the downturn.

According to the study, the impact of this recession on women is shaped by three major factors. First, the significant increases in the number of women in employment over the past thirty years means that women are more directly exposed as employees to the impact of the current recession than ever before. Second, the narrowing of the gender employment gap, combined with the increase in the proportion of lone mother households, means that a woman's wages are more important than ever to the family economy. The percentage of families headed by a single mother has tripled during the past thirty years from seven percent in 1971 to twenty-two percent today (ONS 2008). Among women in relationships, the latest available data shows a woman's income makes up a third of the family income on average and in over a fifth of couples (twenty-one percent) women's incomes account for half of the family income (Women and Equality Unit 2006). Therefore, more families will rely on a woman's wages for their welfare through this recession. Third, women and men enter this recession on an unequal footing. Although there have been major increases in the number of employed women during the past thirty years, the nature of a woman's employment remains markedly different from a man's, and their employment experiences are shaped by motherhood and other caring duties, concentration in particular sectors of the economy, and the traditional undervaluation of women's jobs. A woman's working patterns make her, in most accounts, more economically vulnerable than men from the outset, but the recession does not affect employment alone. The recession will have a broader set of social and economic consequences, some of which will unravel only slowly. A number of factors make women less likely to be able to withstand the impact of the recession. Women are more likely to live in poverty, especially in old age, have fewer financial assets. They are more likely to manage a household budget and act as shock absorbers when this changes, are more likely to experience violence, and as mothers and caregivers will need to make a complex set of decisions about their family and work life influenced by, among other things, the cost of childcare and the tax and benefit system, and other areas.

In 2008, Sen. Ted Kennedy and the Senate Health, Education, Labor and Pensions Committee released a report that examined the effect of economic recession on women. "These findings demonstrate the severe and disproportionate impact of this recession on women and their families. We need to act immediately to restore women's right to fair pay, provide workers with paid sick days, and shore up programs that help workers and families endure hard times," Kennedy said.

The report found that the unemployment rate is rising faster for women than men. Unemployment claims jumped twenty percent for women in March 2008 compared to seventeen percent for men. In 2007, women suffered a larger decline in wages than men. Male workers' wages dropped by half a percent compared to 3% for female workers. Women are also more at risk to lose their homes since they are 32% more likely to have a subprime mortgage. The report also found that non-married women have 48% less net worth than non-married men, and they are less likely to participate in employer-sponsored retirement saving programs.

In times of recession those who make the least money often are the first to feel the pain. The wage discrepancy between women and men means that households where the primary breadwinner is a woman are the ones likely to be hurt the most by any economic downturn. I believe that the Kennedy report highlights the need for urgent action.

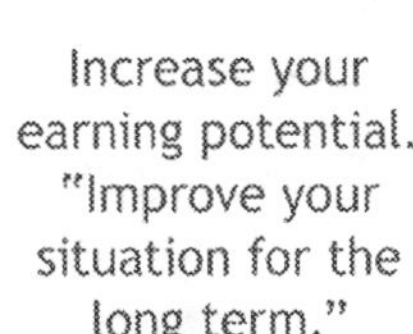

Increase your earning potential. "Improve your situation for the long term."

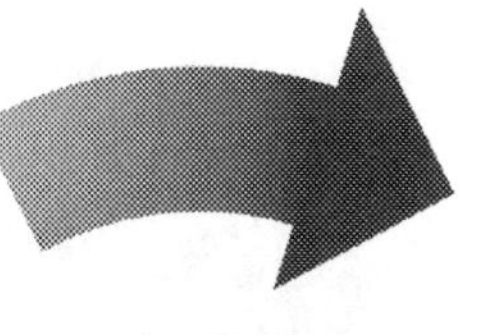

Pay down bad debt and redirect capital into your savings. "Sacrifice today for what you want tomorrow."

"YOUR BAILOUT" Design your own financial intervention plan to prevent financial collapse.

Create a bailout plan for the long-term. "Create a financial strategy that works for you."

Stop the hemorrhaging. "Stop excessive spending."

What is the bailout plan?

Emergency Economic Stabilization Act of 2008

The Emergency Economic Stabilization Act of 2008, commonly referred to as a bailout of the U.S. financial system, was enacted in response to the global financial crisis of 2008 authorizing the United States Secretary of the Treasury to spend up to $700 billion to purchase distressed assets, especially mortgage-backed securities, and make capital injections into banks. Both foreign and domestic banks are included in the bailout. The Federal Reserve also extended help to American Express, whose bank-holding application it recently approved. Treasury Secretary Henry Paulson proposed the Act during the global financial crisis of 2008.

The original proposal was three pages, as submitted to the United States House of Representatives. The plan's purpose was to purchase bad assets, reduce uncertainty regarding the worth of the remaining assets, and restore confidence in the credit markets. The text of the proposed law was expanded to 110 pages and was put forward as an amendment to H.R. 3997. The amendment was rejected via a vote of the House of Representatives on September 29, 2008, by a margin of 228-205.

On October 1, 2008, the Senate debated and voted on an amendment to H.R. 1424, which substituted a newly revised version of the Emergency Economic Stabilization

Act of 2008 for the language of H.R. 1424. The Senate accepted the amendment and passed the entire amended bill by a vote of 74-25. Additional unrelated provisions added an estimated $150 billion to the cost of the package and increased the size of the bill to 451 pages. (See Public Law 110-343 for details on the added provisions.) The amended version of H.R. 1424 was sent to the House for consideration, and on October 3, the House voted 263-171 to enact the bill into law. President Bush signed the bill into law within hours of its enactment, creating a $700 billion Troubled Assets Relief Program to purchase failing bank assets.

Supporters of the bailout plan argued that the market intervention called for by the plan was vital to prevent further erosion of confidence in the U.S. credit markets and that failure to act could lead to an economic depression. Opponents objected to the massive cost of the sudden plan, pointing to polls that showed little support among the public for bailing out Wall Street investment banks, and claimed that better alternatives were not considered and that the Senate only tried to force the passage of the unpopular but sweetened version of the bailout through the opposing House and was successful in this attempt. Opponents of the rescue plan also argue that since the problems of the American economy were created by excess credit and debt, a massive infusion of credit and debt into the economy only exacerbates the problems with the economy: the bailout infuses credit and debt into the economy but, because the government is creating the money out of thin air, immediately creates more credit and debt

Section I

Assess Your Financial Situation

Hiring a professional financial advisor or planner you trust can help you sift through complicated financial decisions. Your financial complacency can cost you more in the long run and hurt your chances for financial freedom in the future. Your decision to hire a professional to help manage your investments, no matter how large or small, is a positive step in the right direction.

If you want something done…

There is a growing focus on personal financial responsibility and global economic stability.

Millions of homes have been lost to foreclosure because individuals lived in a financial fantasy world and chose to ignore their financial reality. In 2008, we learned that if your neighbor could not afford his/her mortgage and lost his/her home to foreclosure it just might have a direct affect on your net worth. Most homeowners have taken inventory of their financial position only once and that was to qualify for a mortgage. After the house was purchased, many families returned to previous financial habits and behaviors that proved to be detrimental to their financial stability.

Recent reports show that, compared to October 2007, in America the number of mortgage foreclosures has increased by twenty-five percent. Historically, individuals who did not have adequate and steady monthly income along with a minimum 20 percent down payment would not have qualified for a home which was 3, 6, or 10 times their annual net income. This practice limited the number of homes sold, limited mortgages to female consumers, and required a more accurate financial assessment to be conducted prior to lending $100,000, $250,000 and up to $800,000 for the purchase of a home.

This section is not a chapter on the struggling mortgage lending industry but more about the need for personal financial accountability with more truth than fable financial analysis. It is not just the mortgage industry that's suffering today. The automobile, the retail, and the financial services industries are all struggling to stay afloat due to consumer variables. More than ever before, it is evident that the "live within our means" advice is more relevant. What does it mean to live within your means? The only way one can meet that lofty goal is to understand where you are financially. According to Credit Research Foundation, the financial statement analysis is a judgmental process. One of the primary objectives is the identification of major changes in trends, and relationships and the investigation of the reasons underlying those changes. The judgment process can be improved through experience and the use of analytical tools.

Credit Research Foundation's definition makes assessing your finances sound like a major CSI investigation. According to Parone Dinanz, owner of Finance Vue, which is a premier resource for finance information, personal finance is a scary subject for some people because it conjures up all sorts of personal fears regarding budgeting, managing investments, and buying versus renting a home.

But before you can make any decision about your personal money management or take any action regarding your finances, you should obtain a firm understanding of your current financial position. Surprisingly, many people have only a vague idea of how much income they actually bring in each month, how much they actually spend each month, and whether the difference between these amounts is in their favor.

Consequently, the first thing to do is assess your financial situation. Gather all of the information and documents that will give you a picture of your financial position. Tally your net worth, including real estate, superannuation (for example pension or retirement income), monthly income and any other assets. You may be pleasantly surprised by the total. After that, create a budget by listing all of your expenses. Be completely honest, and don't leave anything out. If you cheat on this, you will only be cheating yourself. List everything - including luxury items such as dinners out, cosmetics, magazines and movie tickets.

While a budget is absolutely the first step to taking charge of your personal finances, this is by no means the only step you will need to take. Investigate other services in the marketplace such as electronic bill pay, investment counseling, and hints and tips for financial health. Electronic bill pay, or "BPay" as it is more commonly known, is particularly useful for people who tend to be disorganized or procrastinate. Bill Pay allows you to pay bills electronically by direct withdrawal from your bank account and the transaction is processed immediately. You can even receive your bills by e-mail rather than via snail mail (the U.S. Postal Service).

E-PAY, NO WAY!

Some of you may not feel comfortable with establishing an electronic bill pay system because you are never sure your bank account will have enough funds to meet your monthly expense demands. Some of you may be like my mother, as intelligent as she is, who doesn't like paying bills over the Internet because she doesn't trust the unknown. She simply likes writing her checks every month, licking the stamps and mailing her bills. If you believe you are saving money by purchasing stamps, envelopes, and spending one, two even three hours a month opening, reading, and writing checks each month – you are sorely mistaken. Your personal bailout plan needs an upgrade. I also will demonstrate the efficiency you gain by using a safe electronic bill payment system and processes to meet your monthly obligations while saving yourself valuable time each month. If your income is sufficient enough to meet your needs each month but you still find yourself running short, you need a bailout plan and fast. Allow me to provide some essential tools to help you find the holes and create a course of action to mitigate the overspending. There is a fundamental spending problem that needs to be addressed.

Once you have assessed your budget and established a regular and efficient bill paying system, you might feel that you are brave enough to investigate other areas of personal finance such as investments in stocks and bonds. The Internet can be an invaluable resource, allowing you to thoroughly explore the different options and strategies. Finding all sorts of useful references about investments such as term deposits, managed funds, purchasing stocks and shares, and participating in share clubs will aid you in your task. However, start simple and merely open a short-term savings deposit account so that you can make deposits from your paycheck or bank account each week or month, preferably using direct deposit or automatic withdrawal. This way, in no time at all you will begin saving for your next goal whether it be a car, a holiday, or minor surgery.

In order for your personal financial assessment to be a pertinent launch pad for your plan, it must be honest and accurate. Be honest with yourself! Being honest and upfront can make or break the bank in six, twelve, or eighteen years. Here are some helpful steps to help you prepare, assess, and report your current and accurate financial position without paying someone else commission fees or buying money management software:

- Collect all ATM receipts, check registers, retail receipts, and other expense receipts. Organize them by category, industry, and/or date.

- Collect all income receipts such as check stubs or electronic direct deposit notices.
- Enter transactions in order in a sample budget worksheet (Microsoft.com offers free worksheets, search for templates; or any personal finance money management software that you may have received for free with the purchase of your new laptop or personal computer or your new checking account at your local bank or credit union. Again, it is not necessary to purchase expensive money management software.)
- If you have never seen your monthly checking or savings account statement online, visit your local personal banker and ask her to show you how to access your account and statements online. You can also visit most public libraries that provide access to computers with free secure Internet access and low-cost printing. Then access your statement online and from there you may transfer the data to an Excel spreadsheet, you may download a .pdf copy, or simply print your statement. In seconds you can see all bank statements, which include all of your bank transactions. You should review all statements to ensure you do not miss any paid expenses.

Integrate everything into your budget worksheet. Do not forget the fixed expenses, such as:

-mortgage,

-health insurance premiums,

-auto insurance,

-life insurance premiums,

-or college loan payments.

After the data is entered and the calculations are complete, compare your income and expenses per category to the year before, if applicable, and write a memo on areas where you could improve, areas you're on target, and areas that could be eliminated or enhanced. This process could be conducted every week, month, or quarter. Any longer than that and your data will not be as current as it should be for you to have a realistic assessment of your finances. However, the key to successful analysis is to be consistent and do the work required, don't forget to be honest with yourself.

YOUR INVESTMENT

Pros: Organized finances, realistic assessment of spending, recognize areas of improvement in real-time, and all aid in creating a financial management plan that fits your needs.

Cons: Your learning curve may be steep if you are not familiar with accessing information online or have minimal computer or Internet skills. Collecting source documents, receipts, statements or records is time-consuming.

Time Required: 4 to 8 hours the first time, 1-3 hours subsequently following

Cost: $19 - $100

Section 2

Hire an Expert

Hiring a professional financial advisor or planner you trust can help you sift through complicated financial decisions. Your financial complacency can cost you more in the long run and hurt your chances for financial freedom in the future. Your decision to hire a professional to help manage your investments, no matter how large or small, is a positive step in the right direction.

Your assets are distressed!

If you are like most women, making a hiring decision is a big task you would rather delegate to a subordinate or spouse. In today's turbulent economy filled with trials of swindlers accused of mismanaging innocent investors' life savings many are often leery of financial planners, brokers, and fund managers. However, when it comes to your financial future and enhancing your ability to navigate through current economic turbulence, you need a navigation specialist who is trained to find the way through the financial fog and storms. Perhaps, as a novice in the area of personal finance, you may not need a professional for the long term but simply to get the ship headed north again.

Nicole Jacoby believes, "Not everyone needs a financial planner."

While experts agree it's never too soon to start thinking about your financial future, professional financial planning is generally reserved for those whose income and assets have gone beyond a monthly paycheck. However, there is a wide range of reasons for seeking assistance from a financial planner that you may not have considered. You may not have the time or expertise to assess your own financial situation or you may want to obtain a professional opinion concerning a financial plan you developed. You may have an unexpected life event, such as a birth, inheritance, or major illness, which you need to know how to deal with. Or you may want to improve your current financial situation but don't know where to start. "People often confuse financial planning with investing, but financial planning is much broader than that," said Noel Maye, spokesman for the Certified Financial Planner Board of Standards. "Financial planning relates to what kind of a life you want to lead.

While investing may be one element of that, financial planning may also include buying a home, caring for an aging parent or funding a child's college education. Financial planning also helps prepare you for significant life changes, such as a long-term disability, retirement or death of a loved one."

If you think the task of finding, interviewing, and selecting a financial advisor or planner a tad bit daunting, try researching the local paper or community newsletter. Find three names of professionals involved in your community and who work for a reputable firm or institution that shares your values and outlook on community living.

After you have collected three to four names from your local resources, make a few calls to local associates, peers and friends and investigate whether the identified professionals have a solid reputation. Inquire about their expertise and commitment to their field. Sometimes, what is good for John may not fit for Jane. A checklist is provided to help guide you through the interview process.

YOUR INVESTMENT

Pros: Professionally managed portfolio, a professional financial plan, and consistent follow up and access to qualified research and management tools

Cons: Be careful, not all professionals are equal - make sure you find a reputable professional with a solid history and clean background. See resources for tools to conduct background chks.

Time Required: 1-8 hours of research, 1-12 hours of subsequent interview process

Cost: $0 (however, commission fees and management fees may apply)

Checklist for Interviewing a Financial Planner

Planner's Name: ______________________________

Company: ______________________________

Address: ______________________________

Phone: ____________________ Date: ________________

1. Do you have experience in providing advice on the topics below? If yes, indicate the number of years.

- ❑ Retirement planning
- ❑ Investment planning
- ❑ Tax planning
- ❑ Estate planning
- ❑ Insurance planning
- ❑ Integrated planning
- ❑ Other

2. What are your areas of specialization? ________________

____

What qualifies you in this field? ________________

____

3. a. How long have you been offering financial planning advice to clients?

- ❑ Less than one year
- ❑ One to four years
- ❑ Five to 10 years
- ❑ More than 10 years

b. How many clients do you currently have?

- ❑ Less than 10 clients
- ❑ 10 to 39
- ❑ 40 to 79
- ❑ 80 +

4. Briefly describe your work history. ________________

____

5. What are your educational qualifications? Give area of study.

- ❏ Certificate
- ❏ Undergraduate degree
- ❏ Advanced degree
- ❏ Other

6. What financial planning designation(s) or certification(s) do you hold?

- ❏ Certified Financial Planner™ or CFP®
- ❏ Certified Public Accountant/Personal Financial Specialist (CPA/PFS)
- ❏ Chartered Financial Consultant (ChFC)
- ❏ Other

7. What financial planning continuing education requirements do you fulfill? ______________________________

____

8.What licenses do you hold?

- ❏ Insurance
- ❏ Securities
- ❏ CPA
- ❏ J.D.
- ❏ Other

9. a. Are you personally licensed or registered as an Investment Adviser with the:

- ❏ State(s)?
- ❏ Federal Government?
- ❏ If no, why not?

b. Is your firm licensed or registered as an Investment Adviser with the:

- ❏ State(s)?
- ❏ Federal Government?
- ❏ If no, why not?

c. Will you provide me with your disclosure document Form ADV Part II or its state equivalent?

- ❏ Yes
- ❏ No
- ❏ If no, why not?

10. What services do you offer? ______________________

____

11. Describe your approach to financial planning. ________

____

12. a. Who will work with me?

- ❏ Planner
- ❏ Associate(s)

b. Will the same individual(s) review my financial situation?

- ❏ Yes
- ❏ No
- ❏ If no, who will?

13. How are you paid for your services?

- ❏ Fee
- ❏ Commission
- ❏ Fee and commission
- ❏ Salary
- ❏ Other

14. What do you typically charge?

a. Fee:

- ❏ Hourly rate $ ________
- ❏ Flat fee (range) $ ________ to $ ________
- ❏ Percentage of assets under management ________ %

b. Commission:

What is the approximate percentage of the investment or premium you receive on:

- ❑ stocks and bonds ________
- ❑ mutual funds ________
- ❑ annuities ________
- ❑ insurance products ________
- ❑ other ________

15. a. Do you have a business affiliation with any company whose products or services you are recommending?

- ❑ Yes
- ❑ No Explain: ________________________________

b. Is any of your compensation based on selling products?

- ❑ Yes
- ❑ No Explain: ________________________________

c. Do professionals and sales agents to whom you may refer me send business, fees or any other benefits to you?

- ❑ Yes
- ❑ No

  Explain: ________________________________

d. Do you have an affiliation with a broker/dealer?

- ❑ Yes
- ❑ No Explain: ________________________________

e. Are you an owner of, or connected with, any other company whose services or products I will use?

- ❑ Yes
- ❑ No Explain: ________________________________

16. Do you provide a written client engagement agreement?

- ❑ Yes
- ❑ No

  If no, why not? ________________________________

My mama told me, " You'd better shop around!"

Some women may feel intimidated by the process of hiring a professional money manager or financial advisor to help them hold on to their money. Some may feel that they can read a self-help personal finance book and find all the answers to their money woes. Others, as they read this, may hear the Smokey Robinson song playing in their heads, melodically whispering, "My mama told me. I'd better shop around." It is important that you change your behavior and seek help to break the cycle you have unconsciously created since you started paying your own way.

Asking peers, "So what did you do to become financially independent," or interviewing two, four, or even ten different financial advisors until you find the right one is simply good business. It is like the process some go through to find Mr. Right. Most won't marry the first frog they kiss. Hiring a financial advisor or planner is the precursor to a long-term intimate relationship and requires forethought, purposeful planning, and action. So, don't forget, listen to your mama and make the right decision in choosing the right advisor. Make sure the advisor is the right fit for you.

Section 3

Expand Your Resources

You don't necessarily have to land a promotion to start earning more. Showcasing your talents, and acquiring a few more, will leverage your worth and allow you to move up the career ladder.

By Dana Dratch – Bankrate.com

Don't dive into an empty pool!

Most Americans are finding it harder to make ends meet with increased job layoffs, higher gas prices, and a staggering credit crunch. It is time to stop the financial hemorrhaging and expand your resources. There is no magic or secret source. There is no "get rich quick" scheme. Increasing your income to close the gap in your financial shortfalls comes down to one thing - you must change your circumstances.

Saving more money

Research shows the savings rate in the U.S. has virtually diminished. Only a small number of households are saving a significant portion of their income for future needs. Yes, I am asking you to do more with less. Yes, I am asking you to sacrifice today for tomorrow. History shows that households lived on much less in the 1950's and saved, on average, more than families today with higher incomes. This era has experienced natural disasters like none before that have exposed our vulnerability to financial collapse and debt exposure. Hurricane Katrina exposed this vulnerability to financial collapse when a large number of Americans were unable to evacuate due to the lack of liquid capital, also known as immediate cash, and the lack of credit. The current recession has flushed out households ill prepared for financial volatility with a staggering foreclosure rate, credit crunch, and investment losses. Most women do not have three months' mortgage or rent saved. Most could not miss a paycheck without throwing their complete household budget into a devastating downward spiral. The time is now to take a percentage of your primary and supplemental income (for example child support, alimony, or small business income) and save it in a secure financial account that will provide a little more security for future natural and manmade financial disasters.

IF 2 + 2 = 3 AT THE END OF THE MONTH, SOMEBODY'S NOT EATING!

Some female heads-of-household may find it difficult to save each month because they are coming up short on paying just the necessities each month. As a certified financial educator for more than seven years, I have had more mothers come up to me after a class to state, "This is all great information, I know I should be saving but I simply don't have the money..." Most financial experts would tell those mothers the statistics on having three to six months rent/mortgage saved, importance of having an emergency fund, or how important it is to focus on retirement savings early. But, I am here to tell you those facts will not mean a hill of beans to a single mother struggling to make ends meet and keep a household going on her own. The truth is most women do care a great deal about their personal finances. For the most part, women are the single most important purchasing decision makers today. However, due to fear, lack of resources, time, or financial illiteracy a large percentage of women do nothing when it comes to their finances. When I talk to these women at my classes or workshops I simply tell them that they have to change their behavior.

They have to change their mindset and they have to make up their mind that being financially literate is what they want out of life. The truth is, there isn't a magic trick or scheme that's going to make 2 plus 2 equal 4 at the end of the month. You are either going to have to increase your earnings potential through education, job advancement, or small business success. Some steps will be short-term action items that will yield immediate results and others may take two, four, or ten years to see actual changes in your checking account.

Nevertheless, doing nothing means nothing changes.

Increase your knowledge

Whether you return to college to obtain that associates degree, or complete your bachelor's degree, or secure a license or certificate in a particular field or profession, you are adding to your financial success and your knowledge base. The more you know, the more valuable you are. Integrating valuable experience with invaluable education is a powerful combination. Going back to school or enrolling in a new program will require extra time and sacrifice. However, it is an investment of time and money in your future that will enable you to increase your salary requirements plus get you closer to closing the financial gap that exists today.

The $787 billion stimulus bill passed by Congress will not quickly solve the historic problems besetting the economy, but it could reduce the damage, while providing relief for the unemployed and the uninsured. A higher education tax credit. Parents of college students would be eligible to claim a tax credit of up to $2,500. The credit is more generous than the existing Hope Scholarship Tax Credit, which maxes out at $1,800 and is available only for the first two years of college, says Amy McAnarney, executive director of H&R Block's Tax Institute. The tax credit, which would be available in 2009 and 2010, phases out for single taxpayers with AGI of $80,000 to $90,000 and married taxpayers with AGI of $160,000 to $180,000.

Starting your own

As a SBA certified Small Business Management Counselor for the Dallas Small Business Development Center, I often meet aspiring entrepreneurs with big ideas and dreams but less capital and even less of a solid plan for their dreams. My clients express their top reasons for not creating a solid plan is the amount of time and effort it takes in researching and writing a plan. However, I am a firm believer that a path without a plan is just a dirt road that leads to nowhere. Working to generate an alternate source of income is the American way and another way to close the financial gap you may be experiencing today.

It requires some capital investment, time investment, and a sacrifice today for a better tomorrow. Before you run to your local bank or credit union seeking a loan to launch your big idea. Take the time to create a plan first.

The economic stimulus package will help women business owners by enabling local SBA lenders to loosen the reigns by providing a higher loan guarantee for qualified businesses.

The SBA will temporarily raise guarantees and eliminate fees for borrowers on certain 7(a) loans. A bank issues 7(a) loans, which are partially guaranteed by the SBA, to a small business to support its operations.

Additionally, the SBA has temporarily eliminated fees for borrowers and third-party lenders on its 504 Certified Development Company Loans. These loans offer growing small businesses long-term, fixed-rate financing for major fixed assets, such as land, buildings and machinery, and equipment. These loans are aimed at fostering community development, creating jobs, and encouraging modernization.

How do I apply for these loans?

Borrowers apply for loans directly with their lending institutions, including banks, credit unions, and small business lending companies. The SBA works with thousands of small and large lenders nationwide. Lenders evaluate loan applications under their lending standards and decide whether to:

a) Make the loan through conventional financing – without a SBA guarantee – because the borrower meets their conventional credit standards;

b) Make the loan with a SBA guarantee if the borrower does not meet conventional standards and is eligible for SBA programs; or

c) Decline to make the loan.

What kind of businesses typically receive SBA-backed loans?

Typical 7(a) borrowers are entrepreneurs looking to start, expand, or acquire a small business. In many cases, the applicant may have a strong business idea, management ability, and sound financial projections, but may have a shortfall in collateral to secure a loan or equity to put into the business.

In order to qualify for a SBA 7(a) loan, borrowers must be unable to secure conventional commercial financing on reasonable terms and be a "small business" as defined by SBA size standards. In 2008, of the $18 billion in SBA-backed loans, thirty-five percent went to start-up businesses, nearly thirty-two percent ($5.7 billion) went to minority-owned businesses, and nearly twenty-three percent went to women-owned businesses. The most frequently financed industries in 2008 were services, retail trade, accommodation/food service, construction firms, and manufacturing.

SBA-backed loans are three to five times more likely to be made to minority- and women-owned businesses than conventional small business loans made by banks, according to a recent study by the Urban Institute.

Is there a limit on how much I can apply for?

The maximum loan amount for a 7(a) loan is $2 million. For 504 loans, the loan structures and amounts vary since lenders and borrowers each determine how much equity they are putting into the loan. However, for the SBA portion of the loan, the maximum loan amount is either $2 million or $4 million, depending on the purpose of the loan.

For most purposes, the SBA's maximum guarantee for any borrower remains at $1,500,000, or 75 percent of a $2 million loan.

How soon can I get a loan to help me and take advantage of these new programs?

You can apply immediately to any SBA participating lender to take advantage of these programs.

- Fees will be reduced for 7(a) loans.

- Fees will be eliminated for 504 loans.
- Microloan intermediaries across the country are providing loans of up to $35,000 right now to startup, newly established and growing small businesses.

Lenders will work with the SBA to process and approve these loans. Once a loan officer receives a completed loan package from a lender, the SBA can quickly process applications in a few days.

Start Your Business

Starting a business requires you to complete a number of steps and to make some key decisions. As part of your overall plan, you'll need to select a location, decide on a legal business structure, and obtain the necessary licenses and permits. In addition, determining which financing options will meet your short-term needs and long-term goals are crucial. Within this section, we'll provide information on these topics along with guidance on buying an existing business, copyrighting, and trademark issues, and getting support from an outside expert.

Plan Your Business

- Find a Mentor
- Find the Capital (understand the six sources of capital)
- Buy a Business (do research and due diligence up front to protect yourself)
- Buy a Franchise (make sure you know what is required)
- Name Your Business
- Choose a Legal Structure
- Protect Your Ideas and Inventions
- Get Licenses and Permits
- Pick a Location (a location could be your home until the business grows)

- Lease Equipment (create the cost benefit analysis for leasing versus buying)
- Manage Your Business
- Getting Out (for some the reason to start and grow a business is to eventually sell it)

Steps to starting your own business

Write a Business Plan

First, write a business plan for the new business idea. Even if you started the business one, two, or ten years ago, a business plan is an absolute necessity that should not be skipped or prolonged. If you do not know how to create one or have not taken the time to complete a plan with projected financial statements, I would encourage you to do so immediately. You can use business management consulting services at your local Small Business Development Center, a nonprofit business counseling center, sponsored by Small Business Administration. Most of these services are free. Consider taking a continuing education class at your local college or university. The beautiful benefit is most continuing education classes that meet certain requirements will qualify you for receiving financial aid to pay for the small business course or certificate program. It is not necessary to buy expensive business plan writing software. You can use a word processing application such as Microsoft Word to create a rough draft and ultimately your final business plan. You can also find free templates and business plan writing resources online at www.sba.gov. Regions Bank proves to be a very informative and free online resource.

YOUR INVESTMENT

Pros: Writing a plan is a roadmap to success. It helps you develop premeditated solutions for inevitable challenges all businesses may face. It helps to streamline business processes before making huge cash investment in an idea. Legally structuring the business can help mitigate personal and professional risks and liabilities. Finding adequate capital investment BEFORE launching the business is key to long-term success. Cash is king.

Cons: Writing a business plan is not an easy task. Sure, you could hire a professional business plan writer to write your plan but it wouldn't be "your" plan. Business owners can and should be experts at what they do but they also should be keen business and money managers. Expect to spend extensive hours researching your idea, the target market, and creating a detailed marketing and pricing strategy. This may take weeks or months depending on the type of business you plan to start but it is a critical step to success.

Elements of a Business Plan

1. Cover sheet
2. Statement of purpose
3. Table of contents

I. The Business

A. Description of business
B. Marketing
C. Competition
D. Operating procedures
E. Personnel
F. Business insurance

II. Financial Data

A. Loan applications
B. Capital equipment and supply list
C. Balance sheet
D. Breakeven analysis
E. Pro-forma income projections (profit and loss statements)
F. Three-year summary
G. Detail by month, first year
H. Detail by quarters, second and third years
I. Assumptions upon which projections were based
J. Pro-forma cash flow

III. Supporting Documents

A. Tax returns of principals for the last three years' personal financial statement (all banks have these forms)
B. For franchised businesses, a copy of franchise contract and all supporting documents provided by the franchisor
C. Copy of proposed lease or purchase agreement for building space
D. Copy of licenses and other legal documents
E. Copy of resumes of all principals
F. Copies of letters of intent from suppliers, etc.

Legal Structure

You will want to research which legal structure will work best to protect your personal interests, assets, and minimize commercial risk.

There are five different types of legal structures:

- Sole Proprietorship
- General Partnership or Limited Liability Partnership
- Limited Liability Company
- Corporation or S-Corporation
- Non-Profit Corporation

It's important for you to incorporate your filing fees in your startup budget so that the small fees will not bankrupt your small budget before you open your doors, launch, or expand the business. Once you decide which legal structure fits your needs from a legal and financial standpoint you then file the appropriate forms with the IRS. This will let them know of your formal legal structure so that they can update your Employer Identification Number or EIN records.

You then will need to contact your state's comptroller office to inquire about sales and use tax, franchise tax and any other commercial tax liabilities you will be responsible for through the business. Almost all businesses are required to pay taxes on the sale of tangible products or services sold to the general public. A franchise tax is not a tax for a "franchise business" it is purely the name of a tax on commercial income. The only way you'll know if you're required to pay is to call your state or local comptroller's office.

Describe the nature of your business and ask what your tax liabilities are, what tax returns are required, and their due dates. In addition, ask if you are required to obtain a tax identification number for that office. Your local state tax identification number may differ from the Internal Revenue Services employer identification number, better known as your EIN, in most states they are not the same.

There are four taxing agencies:

- Internal Revenue Service
- State Comptroller
- State Unemployment Office
- Local County or City

Keep good records. Know what tax forms are required and deadlines for submission. All agencies have the ability to seize your funds, freeze your checking accounts, and to withdraw penalties based on what they believe you owe if you do not file. Agencies also can audit you, just like the IRS.

Legal Structure Comparison Chart

LEGAL STRUCTURE COMPARISON CHART

Entity Type	Liability	Taxation	Formation	Corporate Maintenance
Regular C-Corporation	Owners have limited personal liability for business debts.	Owners can split corporate profit among owners and corporation, paying lower overall tax rate. Separate taxable entity. Fringe benefits can be deducted as business expense.	May have an unlimited number of shareholders. More expensive to create than partnership or sole proprietorship.	Shares of stock may be sold to raise capital. Formality requirements (e.g. annual reports, minutes, meetings) are required to maintain corporate status.
S-Corporation	Owners have limited personal liability for business debts.	Income must be allocated to owners according to their ownership interests. Owners can use corporate loss to offset income from other sources. Fringe benefits limited for owners who own more than 2% of shares.	More expensive to create than partnership or sole proprietorship.	More formality requirements than for a limited liability company, which offers similar advantages.
Professional Corporation	Owners have no personal liability for malpractice of other owners. Owners have liability for own acts of malpractice.		More expensive to create than partnership or sole proprietorship. All owners must belong to the same profession.	Formality requirements (e.g. annual reports, minutes, meetings) are required to maintain corporate status.
Nonprofit Corporation		Contributions to charitable corporation are tax-deductible. Fringe benefits can be deducted as business expense.		Formality requirements (e.g. annual reports, minutes, meetings) required to maintain corporate status. Property transferred to corporation stays. If corporation ends, property must go to another nonprofit.

Entity Type	Liability	Taxation	Formation	Corporate Maintenance
Limited Liability Company	Combines a corporation's liability protection and pass-through tax structure of a partnership.	IRS rules now allow LLC's to choose between being taxed as partnership or corporation.	More expensive to create than partnership or sole proprietorship.	Significantly easier to maintain than a corporation.
Professional Limited Liability Company	Members have no personal liability for malpractice of other members; however, they are liable for their own acts of malpractice.		Gives state licensed professionals a way to enjoy those advantages. Members must all belong to the same profession. Not available in all states.	
Sole Proprietorship	Owner personally liable for business debts.	Owner reports profit or loss on his or her personal tax return.	Simple and inexpensive to create and operate. No filing necessary.	
General Partnership	Owner (partners) personally liable for business debts.	Owner (partners) reports profit or loss on his or her personal tax returns.	Simple and inexpensive to create and operate. No filing necessary.	
Limited Partnership	Limited partners have limited personal liability for business debts as long as they don't participate in management.		More expensive to create than general partnership.	General partners can raise cash without involving outside investors in management of business. General partners personally liable for business debts.

Source: *MyCorporation.com*

Business Accounting

Hire an accountant on retainer or have one on hand to answer your accounting questions. Do not skimp on this expense because it is crucial to understand the financial side when operating a business – not just for tax reasons, but because you have to know how much you are making, spending, and where best to invest your money. If you are considering financing for the $10,000 you need from a commercial lender such as a bank or credit union, you will need financial projections, solid personal credit, and some assets to use as collateral. There is no way around these facts.

If you do not know how to create the following financial statements to incorporate into your plan, take classes or hire a reputable accountant to create them with you:

- Start-up capital estimate
- Balance sheet
- Profit & Loss statement
- Cash flow statement
- Return on Investment (ROI)

You will need a personal financial statement, as well as, need to demonstrate your financial viability along with showing the ability to repay. I always tell my clients, "Do not quit your day job. You'll need the alternate income to keep the lights on at home." If that is not the case and you are only running your new business, then developing a steady source of income is priority number one.

Lastly, keeping great financial records will make or break a small business. I suggest using small business accounting software to manage accounts payable (A/P), accounts receivables (A/R), and taxes. If business finance terminology is not your strong suit consider taking a few continuing education courses on the subject or visit the American Management Association's website for self-study books and courses on business finance. Aside from creating and implementing a sound sales and marketing strategy, managing your business finances is your most important goal. There is nothing more important than managing your business finances well!

YOUR INVESTMENT

Pros: You walk away with a sound road map for the future; you have a solid understanding of your business and its potential in the marketplace; and you have thought through the financial pros and cons by creating financial projections.

Cons: You could miscalculate your business's true potential earnings and make costly missteps.

Time Required: 24-100 hours of research; 40 - 200 hours of writing and editing business plan

Cost: $100 and up

DON'T STICK YOUR FINGER INTO THE SOCKET!

Starting a small business is not a task that should be taken lightly. Whether you are starting a side photography business or opening your own restaurant, becoming an entrepreneur is risky business, and with the tightening of commercial lending, it will be even more difficult to secure financing. I have been a small business management counselor for more than six years and have counseled hundreds of idealistic entrepreneurs. In some of them, I could see the passion from the time they sat down in my office. I can identify those who are just testing the waters from a mile away.

When I started my first business, I was green and had zero knowledge about what it really took to start, manage, and sustain a successful business. I didn't seek professional guidance. I didn't take a class to understand the intricacies of managing business finances, and I didn't request legal advice from an attorney. I simply had a gut feeling my idea was great and EVERYBODY would want what I had to sell. Well, after a year of missteps, trial, and error, and a great deal of cash out the window, I had to close and realize I started all wrong. I learned a great deal from my mistakes and vowed never to make those mistakes again; however, that failure did not deter my aspirations for owning my own business. I found a job in that field, made every opportunity a learning experience, and properly prepared myself by writing a plan, seeking advice from a financial advisor, and hiring an attorney to help me navigate the start-up pitfalls.

Section 4

Create Your Own Financial Bailout Plan

Creating a useful personal bailout plan to climb out of your financial black hole will require full commitment, concentration, and consistency. Just like the stealth focus you apply to your annual diet promises your personal finances deserve the same.

It wasn't Noah's idea but you can build your own boat!

Six steps to creating a stronger more functional personal financial plan for women:

1. Acknowledge there is a problem

2. In Section Two we analyzed your financial history
3. Create a step-by-step corrective action plan
4. Acquire the capital
5. Work the plan
6. Re-assess (be consistent)

Acknowledge the Problem

Before you can fix a problem, you first must acknowledge a problem exists. Whether the problem is hyper-consumption, insufficient income, or a natural disaster, you must understand the source of the financial pain. If you are not adequately saving for your retirement, if a flat tire will send your financial position into a downward tailspin, or if you fall short with the bills each month or pay important bills 15, 30, 60 days late, "Houston, we have a problem!" Every day there are people who play hide-and-seek in their minds regarding money. Sometimes women tell themselves they cannot afford to take an evening class at the local college because they have children or they have to pay rent. However, when I look at their bank statements I see $5 purchases for Old Navy tees, weekly $25 fees for manicures, or I'll see a purchase for five new Victoria's Secret bras and panties. Most women will hide the fact that they are redirecting their much-needed cash each week to frivolous purchases.

They are seeking a form of satisfaction that they have not found in their everyday lives. This psychological game we play when the important bills are due or when a decision to invest in the future is needed is damaging. If you are guilty of the, "Oh, well…I can't pay so let's play," mind games then you are not ready to face the music. Once you realize that you are sabotaging yourself with these defeatist thoughts you can then identify the problem and begin working on repairing your personal finances.

Where are you falling short financially?

____

____

Analyze your financial history

Once you have acknowledged that a problem exists, conduct your own financial analysis to assess where your income is going. Take the time to record all transactions for 30, 60, or 90 days. Be vigilant and consistent for accuracy. There are a number of free resources online to assist you in capturing data and creating a tool to assess your expenses and unnecessary spending. We all have unnecessary spending that could be eliminated if we make a conscience effort to do so. In today's fast-paced society most of us do not pay attention to "how" we spend our money. We only realize the end result when we sit down at the computer to pull up our online bank account to see just what we purchased during the month. If we added the many transactions indicated as ATM withdrawals, check card debit purchases, Visa or MasterCard check card credit purchases, or check payments most will quickly see that the "SWIPE" has taken control. The SWIPE is the little angel that sits on your shoulder and talks to you when you are in the store, at the bar during happy hour, or at the amusement park. The SWIPE has a mind of his own and seemingly an unlimited amount of resources that he never seems to bother checking. Most people are guilty of letting the SWIPE take the reigns and lead the way until the resources run low and it is back to reality. Most of my workshop attendees will admit that they don't know where the money went and why they use their ATM check cards so frequently versus cash. It is almost a subconscious economy.

Are you balancing your checkbook and your ATM check card charges in your head? If so, why?

____

____

Create a step-by-step corrective action plan

After you have conducted your own personal financial analysis, which includes identifying your real money problems, and have found the hemorrhaging in your finances, you can create a plan to stop the bleeding and to redirect your capital into more worthwhile activities. In addition, this analysis will help you create a plan for increasing your income to meet your household needs. Whether you are writing a household savings and/or spending plan, a business plan, or an investment plan, each requires the use of historical data and future corrective actions that are realistic and accompanied by achievable milestones or goals. Create a goal. Then apply small and realistic action items or steps underneath that goal that you can do in one day, one week, one month, or a quarter (three months). Keep the short-term goals short and sweet while working to achieve the big picture. If you have ever sat through an employee performance review you know how this will go. Some assessments you like and others you believe your boss is completely off base. However, we sit through them because we know our raise depends on it and will soon follow.

Create four boxes and identify key areas of focus. (See exhibit for example.)

Do you create spending goals in advance?

____

____

CORRECTIVE ACTION PLAN

Areas of Focus	Rank Based on Current Performance Level 1 = Poor 2 = Could Be Better 3 = Good 4 = Great	Corrective Action	Deadline
Earning Potential	1	Get a degree, increase my ability to earn additional income	August 2012
Income	2	Get a second job or start a side business	Tomorrow
Spending	1	Stop paying $70 in late charges on credit cards	Next Month
Savings	2	I could save an extra $70 when I stop paying late fees on credit cards	Tomorrow

Saving a little

Research shows the savings rate in the U.S. has virtually diminished. Only a small number of households are saving a significant portion of their income for future needs. Yes, I am asking you to do more with less. Yes, I am asking you to sacrifice today for tomorrow. History shows that households lived on much less in the 1950's and saved, on average, more than families today with higher incomes. This era has experienced natural disasters like none before that have exposed our vulnerability to financial collapse and debt exposure. Hurricane Katrina exposed this vulnerability to financial collapse when a large number of Americans were unable to evacuate due to the lack of liquid capital, also known as immediate cash, and the lack of credit. The current recession has flushed out households ill prepared for financial volatility with a staggering foreclosure rate, credit crunch, and investment losses. Most women do not have three months' mortgage or rent saved. Most could not miss a paycheck without throwing their complete household budget into a devastating downward spiral. The time is now to take a percentage of your primary and supplemental income (for example child support, alimony, or small business income) and save it in a secure financial account that will provide a little more security for future natural and manmade financial disasters.

There are savings initiatives in the U.S. that are providing cash incentives to individuals who qualify to promote savings. They are called Individual Development Accounts or IDAs. These accounts are matched savings accounts that enable American families to save, build assets, and enter teh financial mainstream.

Could you save an extra dollar a month?

____

____

Create and execute the plan (Execute)

Creating a personal financial plan is a necessary step towards financial independence. Similar to a business plan, it provides a roadmap for navigating through financial pitfalls, negative spending habits, and income shortages that may not seem as obvious when you are balancing your checking account in your head or on the back of your grocery store receipt in the car. It is important to take a look at the numbers, reorganize how, when and what you pay, and write a pledge to yourself of your commitment.

Steps to Creating a Financial Plan

Step 1
Divide your financial life into six categories:

- Assets
- Liabilities
- Property and casualty risk (house, car, personal injury, and such)
- Personal risk (life, health, disability, and so on)
- Education (for you or your children, if applicable)
- Retirement

Step 2: Put a dollar figure on each category.
Step 3: Add all assets, and then add all liabilities.
Step 4: Subtract liabilities from assets to calculate your net worth.
Step 5: Evaluate your lifestyle if your net worth is negative, and investigate ways to pay off debt.
Step 6: Develop ways to build on your existing budget. If your net worth is positive, your priority will be to evaluate your lifestyle, transfer "insurable risk" (see glossary) to insurance companies, and invest more to create more wealth. If your net worth is negative, your priority will be to evaluate your income source(s) and increase your immediate earning potential. There is no magic trick to this. If your income is deficient,

build new sources of income or increase your earning potential.

Personal Financial Information

Table of Contents

Introduction

Developing and maintaining a personal financial plan is essential for you to achieve financial security.

Your personal financial plan is composed of many elements, which inter-relate in a dynamic way as you progress through the various stages of your life.

This information is offered to you with the hope that it may help you in developing and maintaining your personal financial plan by:

- Suggesting a variety of financial planning elements that might be helpful.
- Providing a centralized place where your financial planning information can be maintained.

In the event of an emergency or your death, information can be extremely important. Thus, having everything listed in an organized planner makes things simpler.

When you have completed entering the information, place this binder in a safe location. Make sure that its location is known by at least two other family members or close friends. Do not place it in a safe deposit box. Safe deposit boxes have limited access, which hinders loved ones during times of need.

This information is intended for your general use only. You may want to obtain professional advice from either a lawyer or a certified financial planner regarding your specific financial planning.

Personal Information

Legal Name____
SSN ____________________ Birth Date _________________
Maiden Name (if applicable) __________________________
Place of Birth ______________________________________

Spouse's Name ______________________________________
Maiden Name _______________________________________
SSN ____________________ Birth Date _________________
Place of Birth ______________________________________

Parents:

Name	Relationship	Birth Date
____________________	____________	________
____________________	____________	________

Address ____

❑ Living ❑ Deceased

Name	Relationship	Birth Date
____________________	____________	________
____________________	____________	________

Address ____

❑ Living ❑ Deceased

Name	Relationship	Birth Date
____________________	____________	________
____________________	____________	________

Address ____

❑ Living ❑ Deceased

Siblings or Other Relatives:

Name ____

SSN ____________________ Birth Date ________________

Gender ________ Marital Status ____________________

Address ____

Phone ____

Name ____

SSN ____________________ Birth Date ________________

Gender ________ Marital Status ____________________

Address ____

Phone ____

Name ____

SSN ____________________ Birth Date ________________

Gender ________ Marital Status ____________________

Address ____

Phone ____

Employment History:

Present Employer __________________________________

Department ________________ Phone ________________

Title ____________________ Date Hired ______________

Supervisor ________________ Phone ________________

Retirement Benefits: ❑ Yes ❑ No

Former Employer __________________________________

Address ____

Phone ____

Employment Date: From _____________ To: ___________

Retirement Benefits: ❑ Yes ❑ No

Contact person for benefits ___________________________

Phone ____

Former Employer ______________________________
Address ______________________________
Phone ______________________________
Employment Date: From ____________ To: __________
Retirement Benefits: ❑ Yes ❑ No
Contact person for benefits ______________________
Phone ______________________________

Former Employer ______________________________
Address ______________________________
Phone ______________________________
Employment Date: From ____________ To: __________
Retirement Benefits: ❑ Yes ❑ No
Contact person for benefits ______________________
Phone ______________________________

Salary History:

Year	Annual Salary or Annual Income
____________	____________________
____________	____________________
____________	____________________
____________	____________________
____________	____________________
____________	____________________

* Enter the amount from your annual W2 form

Personal Finance

Financial Institutions:

Name of Financial Institution ____________________
Address ____________________
Phone ____________ Contact Person ____________

	Account #(s)	PIN #
❑ Checking	____________	________
❑ Savings	____________	________
❑ Certificates of Deposit	____________	________
❑ Money Market	____________	________
❑ Credit Card(s)	____________	________
(Lost or stolen card call ____________)		
❑ Credit Card(s)	____________	________
(Lost or stolen card call ____________)		
❑ Credit Card(s)	____________	________
(Lost or stolen card call ____________)		

Name of Financial Institution ____________________
Address ____________________
Phone ____________ Contact Person ____________

	Account #(s)	PIN #
❑ Checking	____________	________
❑ Savings	____________	________
❑ Certificates of Deposit	____________	________
❑ Money Market	____________	________
❑ Credit Card(s)	____________	________
(Lost or stolen card call ____________)		
❑ Credit Card(s)	____________	________
(Lost or stolen card call ____________)		
❑ Credit Card(s)	____________	________
(Lost or stolen card call ____________)		

Location of Safe Deposit Box(es):

Name of Bank ____________________ Box # ______________

Address ____

Phone ____

Contact ____

Location of Key _____________________________________

Contents/Inventory: __________________________________

____

____

____

Loan Information:

Name of Bank/Credit Union ______________________________

Address ____

Phone __________________ Account # ___________________

Contact _________________ Collateral __________________

Loan Term _______________ Payoff Date_________________

Credit Life/Disability Insurance: ❑ Yes ❑ No

Name of Bank/Credit Union ______________________________

Address ____

Phone __________________ Account # ___________________

Contact _________________ Collateral __________________

Loan Term _______________ Payoff Date_________________

Credit Life/Disability Insurance: ❑ Yes ❑ No

Name of Bank/Credit Union ______________________________

Address ____

Phone __________________ Account # ___________________

Contact _________________ Collateral __________________

Loan Term _______________ Payoff Date_________________

Credit Life/Disability Insurance: ❑ Yes ❑ No

Other Financial Information ______________________________

____

____

Insurance Checklist

Health Insurance - Medical, Dental and Vision:

Medical Insurance Company ______________________

❑ Group ❑ Individual

Phone Number ______________________

Policy or Certificate Number ______________________

Plan Name and Type:

❑ Hospitalization

❑ Physician Visits

❑ Prescriptions

Dental Insurance Company ______________________

❑ Group ❑ Individual

Phone Number ______________________

Policy or Certificate Number ______________________

Plan Name and Type ______________________

Vision Insurance Company ______________________

❑ Group ❑ Individual

Phone Number ______________________

Policy or Certificate Number ______________________

Plan Name and Type ______________________

Other Insurance Company______________________

❑ Group ❑ Individual

Phone Number ______________________

Policy or Certificate Number ______________________

Plan Name and ______________________

Prescription Information:

Patient Name ______________________

Medication	Dosage/Frequencies	Doctor	Cost
________	________	________	________
________	________	________	________
________	________	________	________

Life Insurance:

Insurance Company ______________________________

❑ Group ❑ Individual

Phone Number ______________________________

Policy or Certificate Number ______________________________

Type of Coverage ______________________________

Amount of Coverage ______________________________

Beneficiaries ______________________________

Disability/Accident Insurance:

Insurance Company ______________________________

❑ Group ❑ Individual

Phone Number ______________________________

Policy or Certificate Number ______________________________

Type of Coverage ______________________________

Amount of Coverage ______________________________

Beneficiaries ______________________________

Auto Insurance:

Insurance Company ______________________________

❑ Group ❑ Individual

Agent ____________________ Phone # ____________________

Policy or Certificate Number ______________________________

Type of Coverage ______________________________

Vehicle 1 ____________________ VIN ____________________

Vehicle 2 ____________________ VIN ____________________

Recreational Vehicle Insurance:

Insurance Company ______________________________

❑ Group ❑ Individual

Agent ____________________ Phone # ____________________

Policy or Certificate Number ______________________________

Type of Coverage ______________________________

Vehicle 1 ____________________ VIN ____________________

Vehicle 2 ____________________ VIN ____________________

Vehicle 3 ____________________ VIN ____________________

Motorcycle ____________________ VIN ____________________

Homeowners/Renters Insurance:

Insurance Company ______________________________

❑ Group ❑ Individual

Agent______________________________

Phone Number ______________________________

Policy or Certificate Number ______________________________

Type of Coverage ______________________________

Umbrella Policy (General Liability Policy):

Insurance Company ______________________________

❑ Group ❑ Individual

Agent______________________________

Phone Number ______________________________

Policy or Certificate Number ______________________________

Type of Coverage ______________________________

Long-Term Care Insurance:

Insurance Company ______________________________

❑ Group ❑ Individual

Agent______________________________

Phone Number ______________________________

Policy or Certificate Number ______________________________

Type of Coverage ______________________________

Pension & Investment Checklist

Check if information is included

Basic Retirement Plan:

Contact: ______________________________

Phone: ______________________________

E-mail: ______________________________

Retirement estimate can be obtained at: ____________

Retirement Estimate Enclosed: ❑ Yes ❑ No

Payout option ______________________________

Beneficiary ______________________________

Other Pension Plan(s):

Company ______________________________

Address ______________________________

Phone ______________________________

Contact Person ______________________________

Amount ______________________________

Company ______________________________

Address ______________________________

Phone ______________________________

Contact Person ______________________________

Amount ______________________________

Other Pertinent Information:

____

____

____

____

____

____

Savings Programs & Other Savings Plans:

1. Tax Deferred Plan (i.e. 401(k) or 403(b))
Plan Balances can be found at: ______________________
Account Number ______________________
Plan Manager ______________________
PIN Number ______________________
Outstanding loans against 403(b) plan ______________________
Date of Loan______________________
Term of Loan ______________________
Final Payment Due______________________

2. After-Tax Plan
Plan Balances can be found at: ______________________
Account Number (Social Security Number)______________________
Location of Semi-Annual Statements______________________
PIN Number ______________________

3. Defined Contribution Plan
Plan Balances can be found at: ______________________
Account Number (Social Security Number)______________________
Location of Semi-Annual Statements______________________
PIN Number ______________________

3.Capital Accumulation Plan (CAP account)
Plan Balances can be found at: ______________________
Account Number (Social Security Number)______________________
Location of Semi-Annual Statements______________________
PIN Number ______________________

4. Other Employer Savings Plans
Plan Balance can be found at: ______________________
Account Number (Social Security Number)______________________
Location of Semi-Annual Statements______________________
PIN Number ______________________

5. Other Employer Savings Plan
Plan Balance can be found at: ______________________
Account Number (Social Security Number)______________
Location of Semi-Annual Statements__________________
PIN Number ___________________________________

Mutual Funds:
Company_____________________________________
Address _____________________________________
Phone ______________________________________
Contact Person_______________________________
Account Number ______________________________

Company_____________________________________
Address _____________________________________
Phone ______________________________________
Contact Person_______________________________
Account Number ______________________________

Stocks and Bonds:
Brokerage Firm ______________________________
Address _____________________________________
Phone ______________________________________
Contact Person_______________________________
Account Number ______________________________

Other Investment Information:
____
____
____
____
____
____

Social Security Information:

Beginning in 2000 the Social Security Administration sends out annual statements to all wage earners. This Personal Earnings and Benefit Estimate Statement shows your Social Security earnings history and estimates how much you have paid in Social Security taxes. It also estimates your future benefits and tells you how you can qualify for benefits. It is a good idea to review these statements for accuracy, and it is important to keep these statements in your records.

General Information and Services:
Hours 7 a.m. to 7 p.m.
(800) 772-1213
http://www.ssa.gov

Tangible Assets Checklist:

Residential Property:

Primary Residence ____________________

Mortgage Holder ____________________

Address ____________________

Phone ____________________

Location of papers (deed, insurance, etc.) ____________

Secondary Residence ____________________

Mortgage Holder ____________________

Address ____________________

Phone ____________________

Location of papers (deed, insurance, etc.) ____________

Other Real Property ____________________

____

____

____

Automobile(s):

Make/Model ____________________

Lien holder ____________________

Address ____________________

Phone ____________________

Insurance Company ____________________

Location of Title ____________________

License Plate # ____________ VIN ____________

Make/Model ____________________

Lien holder ____________________

Address ____________________

Phone ____________________

Insurance Company ____________________

Location of Title ____________________

License Plate # ____________ VIN ____________

Recreational Vehicle(s):

Make/Model ____________________
Lien holder ____________________
Address ____________________
Phone ____________________
Insurance Company ____________________
Location of Title ____________________
License Plate # ____________ VIN ____________

Make/Model ____________________
Lien holder ____________________
Address ____________________
Phone ____________________
Insurance Company ____________________
Location of Title ____________________
License Plate # ____________ VIN ____________

Personal Property:

List all possessions that are valuable, tangible property. Examples: Jewelry, Furniture, Collectibles/Antiques, Home Office Equipment, Electronics, Other Equipment, Books, CD's, Artwork, Musical Instruments, etc.

	Item	Value	Insured Y or N
1.			
2.			
3.			
4.			
5.			
6.			
7.			
8.			
9.			

Location ____________________
____
____

Business Interest(s):

____

____

____

Check if information is included:

- ❑ Limited Partnership
- ❑ General Partnership
- ❑ Sole Proprietorship
- ❑ LLC
- ❑ Corporation
- ❑ Royalties/Residuals
- ❑ Other

Be sure to enclose all pertinent information regarding your additional business interest(s).

Tax Information:

Tax Service Used: ❑ Yes ❑ No

Name of Service ______________________________

Address ______________________________

Contact Person ______________ Phone ____________

Location of Tax Records ______________________

____

____

Charitable Contributions:

Name of Organization ______________________

Annual Donation Amount ____________________

Instructions for Future Donations ______________

____

____

Name of Organization ______________________

Annual Donation Amount ____________________

Instructions for Future Donations ______________

____

____

Wills/Trusts/Estate Planning

Wills and living trusts are legal documents that determine how your estate will be distributed following your death. In the absence of such documents, your property will be distributed among your heirs as prescribed by statute. Because this distribution is unlikely to match your own preferences, you should carefully consider creating a will, a trust, or both. Because estate planning is a complex issue, you should seek appropriate legal counsel to determine how best to meet your individual estate planning requirements.

Attorney for Will ______________________________
Phone ______________________________
Date of Will ______________________________
Location of Will ______________________________
Location of Additional Copies______________________________
Executor ______________________________
Address ______________________________
Phone ______________________________

Attorney for Trust ______________________________
Phone ______________________________
Name of Trust______________________________
Date of Trust______________________________
Trustees ______________________________
Location of Trust Documents ______________________________
Location of Additional Copies______________________________
Trustee Bank (if applicable) ______________________________
Address ______________________________
Phone ______________________________
Contact ______________________________

Acquire the Capital

Minimize your debt and household expenses. Increase your earning potential. Start your own business or get a better paying job.

Your sources for immediate capital are either one of the following or a combination:

- Wages or salary
- Personal or commercial loan from a third party (this infers repayment and added debt on your financial plan's liabilities column)
- Sale of assets
- Interest or dividends earned on investment
- A financial gift

Tax credits for immediate one-time infusion of lump sum cash

The EITC is a refundable federal tax credit for low- and modest-income workers and is one of the most effective tools for lifting families out of poverty. With growing numbers of working families struggling against the rapid downturn in the economy, it is especially important that all eligible families and individuals know about the EITC and how to take full advantage of it. According to CDF's analysis of Internal Revenue Service (IRS) data, in tax year 2006, more than 22 million taxpayers received the EITC, with an average benefit amount of $1,950. According to the Center on Budget and Policy Priorities, the most recent estimates show that the EITC lifted 4.4 million low-income Americans out of poverty–including 2.4 million children.

According to the IRS, a tax credit usually means more money in your pocket. It reduces the amount of taxes you owe. If you are a single female head of household with two or more minor dependents and earn less than $40,000, chances are you qualify for a tax credit that could provide a much-needed, one-time cash infusion at tax time.

Earned Income Tax Credit

The earned income credit (EITC) is a tax credit for certain people who work and have low wages. A tax credit usually means more money in your pocket. It reduces the amount of tax you owe. The EITC may also give you a refund.

Earned income includes all the taxable income and wages you gain from working.

There are two ways to receive earned income:

You work for someone who pays you, or; you work in a business you own.

Taxable earned income includes:

Wages, salaries, and tips;

Union strike benefits;

Long-term disability benefits received prior to minimum retirement age;

Net earnings from self-employment.

You may prefer to receive some of next year's EITC throughout the year, rather than wait and get EITC after you file your tax return. To get EITC, complete Form W-5 and give the lower part of the form to your employer. Keep the top part for your records.

Unfortunately, like itemized deductions, charitable donations, mortgage deductions and other tax benefits, 401(K) investments are not designed to benefit low-income clients. If you owe no taxes, you receive no direct benefit from reducing your taxable income as do people who are in the twenty-eight percent tax bracket. Also, we see so many low-income workers withdraw their 401(K) early and have to pay taxes plus the ten percent penalty. Anecdotally, for people who don't have savings for emergencies, 401(K) is probably not the best savings vehicle, unless there is an employer match, because of the steep penalty for early withdrawal.

Child Care Credit

This credit is for people who have a qualifying child as defined on the IRS.gov website. It is in addition to the credit for child and dependent care expenses (on Form 1040, line 48; Form 1040A, line 29; or Form 1040NR, line 45) and the earned income credit (on Form 1040, line 64a; or Form 1040A, line 40a). The maximum amount you can claim for the credit is $1,000 for each qualifying child. To claim the child tax credit, you must file Form 1040, Form 1040A, or Form 1040NR. You cannot claim the child tax credit on Form 1040EZ or Form 1040NR-EZ. You must provide the name and identification number (usually a Social Security Number) on your tax return (or Form 8901) for each qualifying child.

Earned Income

You will need to figure your earned income using one of the worksheets on the IRS.gov website or Form 8812. Form 1040 or Form 1040NR filers must use the worksheet on page 8 to determine your earned income. Form 1040A or Form 1040NR must use a different worksheet to determine your earned income.

For this purpose, earned income includes only:

- Taxable earned income
- Nontaxable combat pay

This credit is for certain individuals who get less than the full amount of the child tax credit. The additional child tax credit may give you a refund even if you do not owe any tax.

Tax Credit for First-Time Homebuyer

First-time homebuyers should begin planning now to take advantage of a new tax credit included in the recently enacted Housing and Economic Recovery Act of 2008.

Available for a limited time only, the credit:

- Applies to home purchases after April 8, 2008, and before July 1, 2009.
- Reduces a taxpayer's tax bill or increases his or her refund, dollar for dollar.
- Is fully refundable, meaning that the credit will be paid out to eligible taxpayers, even if they owe no taxes or the credit is more than the taxes that they owe.

However, the credit operates much like an interest-free loan, because it must be repaid over a 15-year period. So, for example, an eligible taxpayer who buys a home today and properly claims the maximum available credit of $7,500 on his or her 2008 federal income tax return must begin repaying the credit by including one-fifteenth of this amount, or $500, as an additional tax on his or her 2010 return.

Eligible taxpayers will claim the credit on new IRS Form 5405. This form, along with further instructions on claiming the first-time homebuyer credit, will be included in 2008 tax forms and instructions and be available later this year on the IRS website, IRS.gov.

If you bought a home recently, or are considering buying one, the following questions and answers may help you determine whether you qualify for the credit.

Tax Credit for Hybrid Cars

The Energy Policy Act of 2005 replaced the clean-fuel burning deduction with a tax credit. A tax credit is subtracted directly from the total amount of federal tax owed, thus reducing or even eliminating the taxpayer's tax obligation. The tax credit for hybrid vehicles applies to vehicles purchased or placed in service on or after January 1, 2006.

The credit is only available to the original purchaser of a new, qualifying vehicle. If a qualifying vehicle is leased to a consumer, the leasing company may claim the credit. Hybrid vehicles have drive trains powered by both an internal combustion engine and a rechargeable battery. Many currently available hybrid vehicles may qualify for the tax credit.

Tax Credit for Energy Efficiency

The Internal Revenue Service reminded individual and business taxpayers that many energy-saving steps taken in 2009 may result in bigger tax savings next year.

The recently enacted American Recovery and Reinvestment Act (ARRA) of 2009 contained a number of either new or expanded tax benefits on expenditures to reduce energy use or create new energy sources. The IRS encouraged individuals and businesses to explore whether they are eligible for any of the new energy tax provisions. More information on the wide range of energy items is available on the special Recovery section of IRS.gov. For a larger listing of ARRA's energy-related tax benefits, see Energy Provisions of the American Recovery and Reinvestment Act of 2009 fact sheet at IRS.gov.

Tax Credits for Home Energy Efficiency Improvements Increase

Homeowners can get bigger tax credits for making energy efficiency improvements or installing alternative energy equipment.

The IRS also announced that homeowners seeking these tax credits can temporarily rely on existing manufacturer certifications or appropriate Energy Star labels for purchasing qualifying products until updated certification guidelines are announced later this spring.

"These new, expanded credits encourage homeowners to make improvements that will make their homes more energy efficient," said IRS Commissioner Doug Shulman. "People can improve their homes and save money over the long run."

ARRA provides for a uniform credit of thirty percent of the cost of qualifying improvements up to $1,500, such as adding insulation, energy-efficient exterior windows, and energy-efficient heating and air conditioning systems. The new law replaces the old law combination available in 2007 of a ten-percent credit for certain property and a credit equal to cost up to a specified amount for other property.

The new law also increased the limit on the amount that can be claimed for improvements placed in service during 2009 and 2010 to $1,500, instead of the $500 lifetime limit under the old law.

In addition, the new law has increased the energy efficiency standards for building insulation, exterior windows, doors, and skylights, certain central air conditioners, and natural gas, propane, or oil water heaters placed in service after February 17, 2009.

You can get free help with your return. Free help in preparing your return is available nationwide from IRS-trained volunteers. The Volunteer Income Tax Assistance (VITA) program is designed to help low-income taxpayers and the Tax Counseling for the Elderly (TCE) program is designed to assist taxpayers age 60 and older with their tax returns. Many VITA sites offer free electronic filing and all volunteers will tell you about credits and deductions you may be entitled to claim. To find the nearest VITA or TCE site, call 1-800-829-1040. As part of the TCE program, AARP offers the Tax-Aide counseling program. To find the nearest AARP Tax-Aide site, call 1-888-227-7669 or visit AARP's website at www.aarp.org/money/taxaide.

If you want to use this one-time cash infusion as a means of establishing that much-needed emergency savings fund, eliminate the need to spend before you receive it. Most adults have pre-spent their tax-refund before they ever file the report. A late medical bill, a new car, a day at Six Flags amusement park with the kids are all excuses I have heard all too often. This refund is an opportunity to start over and begin your new year in the black. Use it wisely. This is a sure-fire way to bail yourself out of the financial hole you have dug.

Re-Assess

After the action plan has been created, keeping in mind this is a living document that will change frequently, it is a good idea to take time to review the plan and compare it to your actual outcomes. It is important to measure whether you met your intended goals, if you exceeded your spending limits, or if you can markedly see a change in your money management behavior on paper. If there are areas you can improve, do it immediately. If there are areas you accomplished your goals, give yourself a pat on the back and a big hug. You did it!

YOUR INVESTMENT

Pros: The human psyche believes that anything we invest valuable resources into such as money or time, we are going to place more value on that product or activity. If you take the time to collect your data, write a complete financial plan, and create a strategy for implementing the plan you are halfway to the promise land. The hard part is making a conscious decision to change your money management habits and behavior; then putting the information on paper with steps to fix the problem. This takes time and dedication that resembles the action steps one may take to lose 30 pounds, but for some the hardest part is getting started.

Cons: Once you sit down to add the numbers you may quickly realize the Titanic is sinking and you are left without a life jacket or boat. Some households are living in denial and as long as we sweep the financial problems under the rug and can afford our weekly lattes or daily cheeseburgers we are blissfully broke. The problem is recognized when you put the problem on paper and realize it is too much to fix. You may want to give up before you start. This is a normal reaction, however, it is not the right solution.

Time Required: 3 - 60 Hours

Cost: $0

NO PAIN, NO GAIN!

Some women heads-of-household may find it difficult to save each month because they are coming up short on paying the necessities each month. As a certified financial educator for more than seven years, I have had more mothers come up to me after a class to state, "This is all great information, I know I should be saving but I simply don't have the money…" Most financial experts would tell these mothers the statistics on having three to six months rent/mortgage saved, the importance of having an emergency fund, or how important it is to focus on retirement savings early. However, I am here to tell you, those facts will not mean a hill of beans to a single mother struggling to make ends meet and keep a household going. The truth is most women do care a great deal about their personal finances. For the most part, women are the single most important purchasing decision makers today. However, due to fear, lack of resources, time, or financial illiteracy, a large percentage of women do nothing when it comes to their finances. When I talk to these women in my classes or workshops, I simply tell them they have to change their behavior. They have to change their mindset, and they have to make up their mind that being financially literate is what they want out of life.

Section 5

Understanding Financial Terminology

To create your own winning bailout plan it is important that you understand basic financial terminology. New terms are created each day and some were introduced in this guide. Here are some of the terms you may run across as you research and implement your new strategy.

Bailout

An instance of coming to the rescue, esp. financially: *a government bailout of a large company.*

Finance

The management of money, banking, investments, and credit.

EIN

An Employer Identification Number (EIN) is also known as a Federal Tax Identification Number, and is used to identify a business entity. Generally, businesses need an EIN.

Debt

Something owed, such as money, goods, or services.

Savings Account

An account that draws interest at a bank. With a savings account you can make withdrawals, but you do not have the flexibility of using checks to do so. Withdrawals are limited.

Investment

The act of investing. An amount invested. Property or another possession acquired for future financial return or benefit. A commitment, as of time or support.

Budget

An estimation of the revenue and expenses over a specified future period of time. A budget can be made for a person, a family or a group of people, a business, government, country or multinational organization or just about anything else that makes and spends money.

Credit

Time allowed for payment for goods or services obtained on trust.

Income

The monetary payment received for goods or services, or from other sources, as rents or investments.

Entrepreneur

A person who organizes, operates, and assumes the risk for a business venture.

Business

The occupation, work, or trade in which a person is engaged: the wholesale food business. A specific occupation or pursuit: the best designer in the business. Commercial, industrial, or professional dealings: new systems now being used in business. A commercial enterprise or establishment: bought his uncle's business. Volume or amount of commercial trade: Business had fallen off. Commercial dealings; patronage: took her business to a trustworthy salesperson.

Financial Plan

A personal financial plan provides strategies for dealing with periods of personal hardship and helps develop a prudent economic agenda for you and/or your family.

Portfolio

The group of assets - such as stocks, bonds and mutual funds - held by an investor. To reduce their risk, investors tend to hold more than just a single stock or other asset. Think of the portfolio as a pie: each piece is divided into specific assets such as bonds, equities, etc.

Accountant

A person whose profession is inspecting and auditing personal or commercial financial accounts.

IRS

Internal Revenue Service - the bureau of the Treasury Department responsible for tax collections.

Comptroller

Variant of "controller" office, which audits accounts and supervises the financial affairs of a governmental body.

Unemployment Tax

The Federal Unemployment Tax Act (FUTA), authorizes the Internal Revenue Service to collect a federal employer tax used to fund state workforce agencies. Employers pay this tax annually by filing IRS Form 940. FUTA covers the costs of administering the UI and Job Service programs in all states. The primary goal of the Unemployment Insurance Tax Division is to provide and account for the funding needed to pay benefits to those individuals who become unemployed through no fault of their own. Unemployed workers can choose to have income tax withheld from their unemployment benefit payments. Withholding on these payments is voluntary. However, choosing this option may help avoid a surprise year-end **tax** bill or a possible penalty for having paid too little **tax** during the year.

Franchise Tax

A tax that is imposed by states on corporations; it depends both on the net worth of the corporation and on its net income attributable to activities within the state

Start-up capital estimate

A calculation of how much money you will need for a start-up business.

Balance Sheet

A statement of the financial position of a business on a specified date.

Profit & Loss Statement

Also called a P&L - A financial statement that summarizes the revenues, costs, and expenses incurred during a specific period of time - usually a fiscal quarter or year. These records provide information that shows the ability of a company to generate profit by increasing revenue and reducing costs. The P&L statement is also known as a "statement of profit and loss," an "income statement," or an "income and expense statement."

Cash Flow Statement

The Cash Flow Statement (CFS), a mandatory part of a company's financial reports since 1987, records the amounts of cash and cash equivalents entering and leaving a company. In business finance it is the receipt of money, generally from sales. In personal finance it is the receipt of money, generally from salary or wages.

Return on Investment

The amount your business profits from its marketing expenditures. The goal of marketing is to increase revenues. A performance measure used to evaluate the efficiency of an investment or to compare the efficiency of a number of different investments. To calculate ROI, the benefit (return) of an investment is divided by the cost of the investment; the result is expressed as a percentage or a ratio. Return on investment is a very popular metric because of its versatility and simplicity. That is, if an investment does not have a positive ROI, or if there are other opportunities with a higher ROI, then the investment should be not be undertaken.

The return on investment formula:

$$ROI = \frac{(\text{Gain from Investment} - \text{Cost of Investment})}{\text{Cost of Investment}}$$

Collateral

Property acceptable as security for a loan or other obligation.

RESOURCES

http://www.investopedia.com

http://www.investorwords.com

http://www.SBA.gov

http:www.recovery.gov

http://www.grants.gov

http://www.360financialliteracy.org

http://www.singlemothersbychoice.com

http://www.wife.org

http://www.feedthepig.org

http://www.americasaves.org

http://www.jrfinance.com

http://www.geezeo.com

http://www.wiseupwomen.org

http://www.msmoney.com

http://www.ssa.gov

http://www.widowswithwisdom.org

http://www.amanet.org

http://www.regions.com/small_business/business_resource_center.rf.

http://www.dcccd.edu

http://www.cynthianevels.com

http://www.financialstability.gov
http://www.ingdirect.com
http://www.philanthropy.ml.com
http://www.cfed.org
http://www.financialbailoutguide.com

About the Author

Cynthia E. Nevels is president of CynthiaNevels.com and the host of C-CASTS. She is a certified financial educator, certified small business management counselor, and certified entrepreneurship professor.

She is the founder of Jr. Finance Literacy Academy, Inc. one of the fastest growing nonprofit financial education enrichment service providers in the United States.

She believes teaching children the importance of money management is important to the global economy in the long term. She is the mother of three children and dedicates her life to mentoring children and adults on the importance of financial literacy and asset building.